D●N'T
PANIC

D**N**'T PANIC

HOW *to* MANAGE *your* FINANCES *and* FINANCIAL ANXIETIES DURING *and* AFTER CORONAVIRUS

Christine Ibbotson,

Licensed Financial & Investment Advisor,
Estate Planner, and Tax Specialist

NIMBUS
PUBLISHING
— NIMBUS.CA —

Nimbus Publishing Limited
3660 Strawberry Hill Street, Halifax, NS, B3K 5A9
(902) 455-4286 nimbus.ca

Printed and bound in Canada
NB1550

Edited by Angela Mombourquette
Design by Heather Bryan

Library and Archives Canada Cataloguing in Publication
Title: Don't panic : how to manage your finances — and financial anxieties —
during and after coronavirus : tips, tricks, and guaranteed ways to secure your
future / Christine Ibbotson, Licensed Financial Advisor.
Other titles: Do not panic : how to manage your finances — and financial anxiet-
ies — during and after coronavirus : tips, tricks, and guaranteed ways to secure
your future | How to manage your finances — and financial anxieties — during
and after coronavirus : tips, tricks, and guaranteed ways to secure your future |
Tips, tricks, and guaranteed ways to secure your future
Names: Ibbotson, Christine, author. Identifiers: Canadiana (print) 20200213458
| Canadiana (ebook) 20200213482 | ISBN 9781771089050 (softcover) |
ISBN 9781771089043 (HTML) Subjects: LCSH: Finance, Personal—
Handbooks, manuals, etc. | LCSH: Retirement—Planning—Handbooks, man-
uals, etc. | LCGFT: Handbooks and manuals. Classification: LCC HG179 .I23
2020 | DDC 332.024—dc23

Nimbus Publishing acknowledges the financial support for its publishing activities from the Government of Canada, the Canada Council for the Arts, and from
the Province of Nova Scotia. We are pleased to work in partnership with the
Province of Nova Scotia to develop and promote our creative industries for the
benefit of all Nova Scotians.

CONTENTS

PANDEMIC PANIC— IS THIS REALLY HAPPENING?

IN A SCENARIO THAT COULD BE STRAIGHT OUT OF A MOVIE, COVID-19 (the disease caused by the novel coronavirus) has become a worldwide pandemic that is leaving people feeling panicked and displaced. We have all seen the empty grocery store shelves, with some banks even running out of cash because so many people have made withdrawals. Many people are in a state of near-hysteria—and how can we blame them? Information about the spread of the virus keeps changing by the hour. With a constant stream of social media and news updates, many of us are feeling overwhelmed.

As the virus is transmitted to more and more people, we may see our social infrastructure become even more strained.

With the exception of essential services, businesses large and small have closed their doors. All bars, restaurants, theatres, sport and concert venues have been shut down, and live performances cancelled. To add to this, all schools, daycares, and child care centres have also been closed, forcing parents to scramble. Governments worldwide have recommended social distancing and have told us to "just stay home."

So how did this happen?

The world witnessed the first outbreak in the bustling commercial city of Wuhan, China, where it is believed that an animal-to-human transmission may have occurred at a live animal market in December 2019. On December 31, 2019, China alerted the World Health Organization to several cases of an unusual pneumonia in Wuhan, and on January 11, 2020, Chinese state media reported the first known death from an illness caused by the virus. (A scientific paper published in January 2020 challenged the idea that the virus first surfaced at that market, suggesting that it may have spread between people in Wuhan—and perhaps elsewhere—before that cluster of cases was discovered in late December.)

The virus was being spread person-to-person. As the pandemic quickly grew, by March 25, 2020, there were more than 430,000 reported cases worldwide, and that number was growing exponentially every day. More than 160 countries and every continent except Antarctica has been affected.

According to the US Centers for Disease Control and

Prevention, the virus is thought to be spread mainly via the droplets that are produced when an infected person coughs or sneezes on someone who is within about two metres of them. Some spread might be possible before infected people show symptoms, but that's probably not the main way the virus spreads. It may also be possible that a person can get COVID-19 by touching a surface or object that has the virus on it and then touching their own mouth, nose, or eyes, but this also isn't thought to be the main way the virus spreads.

Washing our hands and disinfecting surfaces have become common practices as the virus continues to spread. We are inundated with daunting news stories, and "How to properly wash your hands" has become a major topic in the media. Because so many people are in self-solation or are practicing social distancing, some towns, villages, and even cities appear empty, creating a sense of ghostly eeriness.

We now see countries closing their borders, banning air travel, and in some cases denying entry to anyone who is not a citizen or permanent resident—steps that had previously been considered a last resort.

Research into a vaccine is ongoing, but for many, it can't come soon enough, especially for those most in need. People with chronic medical conditions, weakened immune systems, and older people are at the greatest risk of dying if they become infected.

Many of us who suddenly have all this extra time on our

hands are wondering what to do about money. How will we pay our rent or mortgage, and how can we put food on the table? What happens if we get sick, too? We are told that our hospitals may be overwhelmed by the greater demand, and that other sectors such as law enforcement, supply chains, medical services, and transportation could be severely affected.

The cancellation and curtailment of public activities to mitigate the impact of this virus is having a tremendous impact on business, commerce, and financial markets. We are now facing a potential global financial crisis and—dare I say— an imminent recession.

Are You Worried About Making the Rent?

Today the majority of people live paycheque to paycheque, and worrying about personal finances can create a lot of anxiety—especially now that we have to deal with the COVID-19 pandemic.

As the pandemic continues, some fortunate people will be able to keep earning income as they work from home. But for others there is more uncertainty. If your employer is a small business that plans to stop paying you during this time, or if you are self-employed, on contract, or generally work for cash—what will you do?

I am pleased to see that governments are stepping up in this crisis to protect workers as well as business owners. Governments have funnelled billions of dollars into our financial systems to ensure that banks can continue to lend, and banks have been encouraged to suspend mortgage payments for customers over the next few months. If you live in Canada, the US, or the UK, your governments have ensured that lending institutions and large banks can provide a three- to six-month mortgage and loan suspension for their customers. This is further supported by governments lowering their central bank rates to ensure that lenders keep interest rates low for future borrowing.

If you have a home with a mortgage, chances are you will be given a "payment holiday" for a couple of months to make things easier for your family's budget, but be careful to read the fine print. Most banks and lending institutions are not providing free "time off" from your loans. Even though you are not required to make your payment for a few months, interest will continue to accrue on the outstanding balance. Another thing to remember is that this is not a long-term solution, and if you are looking to improve your overall cash flow you may want to take advantage of the low–lending-rate environment and refinance your debt (more on this in Chapter 2).

While this is great for homeowners, what happens to those who are paying rent? How will they make ends meet month to month? This could be a real problem for people who are now in a compromised income situation and who still have to pay rent and put food on the table. Short of getting a personal loan or a line of credit, what else can these folks do to make ends meet? Understandably, renters are worried about their landlords evicting them if their income is reduced due to the coronavirus crisis.

Fortunately, governments have again been quick to act, and I can't stress enough how great this is. As of the writing of this book, the UK, most of the US, and some provinces in Canada have instituted executive orders that put a moratorium on evictions for thirty to sixty days in order to protect the millions of people who work in hourly or lower-waged employment and who are finding making ends meet stressful. Again, this is not a long-term solution, but it does take some of the stress off those who may find paying rent particularly difficult at this time. The last thing anyone wants is to have families become homeless, and it seems like our governments are working to ensure that this doesn't happen.

What Can We Learn from the Past?

It has only been twelve years since the financial crisis that rocked the world economy. In 2008 we saw many people lose their jobs, homes, retirement savings—and basically their will to keep fighting through those troubled times. Massive monetary bailouts and unprecedented fiscal stimulus packages were needed to prop up financial systems worldwide, and we saw a rapid global economic downturn. Combined with the US sub-prime crisis and the European debt crisis, stock markets around the world were decimated in a matter of weeks. The credit freeze nearly brought the global financial system to a full-scale collapse, and many governments had to absorb the banks' debts and institute large-scale monetary actions. Real estate prices dropped and we saw people in the US hand over their keys and walk away from their homes, which were suddenly worth less than their mortgages.

It was a terrible time in our history and many people today are still feeling the scars left by that great financial breakdown. But a lot of good came out of that recession. Our stock market quadrupled in value from 2009 to 2019, so if you had been brave enough to invest when the market was tanking, you would have made four times your investment. (A possible stock market déjà vu opportunity will be discussed further in Chapter 2.)

Over the last ten years, we have seen great moves to ensure that history does not repeat itself, with governments and financial institutions far more cognizant of their obligations. Stringent lending and adjudication rules have been established and regulatory bodies are continuously updating those rules to ensure that such a crisis never happens again, creating a solid financial system with consumer protection.

Today's pandemic is not the same as that financial crisis, and in a way, it is good that we had that crisis first, since our governments are now quicker to react to support families by providing job security and debt coverage. Governments are also protecting industry, corporations, and small business by extending credit, waiving fees, and encouraging, and in some cases mandating, employers to support their staff. Many governments have even gone a step further to ensure that no employee can be fired or laid off, regardless of their prior arrangement, and regardless of whether they were on probation or employed as a part-time or seasonal worker.

The Canadian, US, and UK governments have also reduced the wait times to get unemployment insurance benefits, and Canada and the US have even delayed the personal income tax filing deadlines.

Getting to Know Your True Costs

Now that you know that banks and governments are offering you some protection, let's look at what you can do to ensure you have a viable plan to get through these uncertain times.

It is always a good practice to track your monthly expenditures. Perhaps being forced to be accountable now—and given that you likely have a little extra time—you can determine what those true costs are. Creating a budget to monitor daily and monthly cash flow is an excellent step toward finding ways to trim your lifestyle costs.

First, let's make a list of all the expenditures you will be facing over the next few months so you can see what you are really dealing with. Once this is done, you can then begin to develop new strategies to trim down any costly expenses and create a stronger monthly cash flow.

Rent or mortgage payment	$	Monthly payment
Property taxes	$	Monthly payment
Condo/maintenance fees	$	Monthly payment
Hydro	$	Monthly payment
Water/sewer	$	Monthly payment
Gas/propane/heating	$	Monthly payment
Car lease/loan	$	Monthly payment
School loans, other	$	Monthly payment
Debts, credit cards, loans	$	Minimum payments only
Food and other	$	Calculate your average monthly food budget + 15% to stock up on extras you need
Alimony/child support	$	Monthly payment
Takeout meals	$0	Cut these out for now, please!
Entertainment	$0	Since everything is closed, looks like it's just a bag of popcorn and Netflix!
Total monthly costs to budget:	$	

Now, knowing what you need to account for each month, do you have enough money to cover these expenses? Do you need to look at government assistance or can you tap into your savings to make up for the shortfall? Sometimes all it takes is a few simple changes to become less wasteful. Remember that your greatest source of more money is your own earning potential. Never underestimate your inherent ability to succeed.

Why not take this opportunity to consider new opportunities with your current employer? Become inspired by reading about successful people and keep a journal to keep you on track, encouraged, and motivated.

How to Improve Your Cash Flow During the Crisis

Banks and financial institutions are considered essential services like grocery stores and pharmacies, so they will remain open during the coronavirus crisis. We have been told that most lending institutions may cut back on their opening hours or may close up to 20 percent of their branches, but they will still be open for business and will have a full offering of services online, in addition to those at their physical locations.

If you are concerned about cash flow, your bank has a couple of options that can improve it. Most conventional mortgages have a "skip-a-payment" option. This allows those mortgagors who are in good standing to skip one mortgage payment per calendar year. All the large tier-one banks also have embedded cash accounts on their conventional mortgages that clients can access to either skip payments or withdraw funds in times of need.

You should also use this low-rate environment to review your debt portfolio. Regardless of when your mortgage is up for renewal, why not consider refinancing your mortgage, consolidating debt, or doing an equity takeout to increase cash flow and to invest? If you don't have a mortgage, you could talk to your bank to see if you can get a line of credit, a lower rate on a restructured loan, or even an overdraft on your bank account to tide you over until things recover.

These sorts of steps should not be viewed as a financial weakness or a plan to get into more debt, but rather as good financial planning to ensure you are equipped for future uncertainties, and to ensure the stability of your monthly cash flow. You should always be looking for opportunities to reduce your risk. Refinancing your mortgage to capture a lower rate is not a bad thing. Let me be clear: if you did it all the time, it would not be good! But with the rates now dropping even lower than they were before the crisis, it definitely makes sense to revisit your debt portfolio and see if you can save on future interest.

If you plan to refinance your debt, and plan on taking a new loan, please do not opt for the longest amortization. The amortization should be set to match the number of years you have left until you turn sixty-five. For example, if you are forty-five years old, the amortization on your new mortgage loan should be twenty years. You want to start making decisions based on the bigger picture and as a plan for the future. Remember that you want to get rid of this debt by retirement, so please do not extend the loan past that future date.

How Can You Accomplish More?

Your ability to come through this crisis or any future predicament will greatly depend on your resolve and your ability to take ownership of your financial situation. The primary challenge in creating wealth is saving, and for most of us this is a difficult task when we have so many demands on our money. In Chapter 4, I am going to show you how to create true financial independence using a technique called a "cascading financial plan," but for now all you need to know is that there are only three tasks you need to master to become wealthy.

Think of this approach as a three-legged stool: if you are missing one leg, the stool topples over. You must have all three legs working together to be successful. No matter where you are in life or what you do for a living, if you want to eventually retire comfortably you must have these three things:

1. Earnings
2. Accumulation and savings
3. The ability to build wealth over time through monetization and growth.

The first two steps are self-explanatory and the third is defined by the placing of your savings into an asset that will grow over time—for example, home ownership, a stock portfolio, or an investment.

Most people already know this concept and are probably doing okay financially, but they still have a love-hate relationship with money. They either believe they don't have enough, they will never have enough and will always need more, or their life would be better if they only had a little extra. Almost everyone is innately unsatisfied with their monetary situation, and I am not here to belabour whether you do or don't need more. The fact is, you need to know what you want out of your life, you need to know what your endgame is, and you need to have a plan for how you envision the rest of your life. Having money or the security it provides will ensure your long-term happiness and comfort as you get older. It is important for you to take ownership of your future now, whatever that future may hold.

Give yourself permission to go in a different direction than the crowd when you are searching for new ways to be successful. Never give up, and never doubt your earning potential. Remember that no one achieves greatness in life without getting out of the ordinary and challenging themselves to attain something more.

DURING AND AFTER THE COVID-19 PANDEMIC

AS I WRITE THIS I AM SEEING CONTINUED COMMITMENTS from governments to do whatever it takes to alleviate the economic fallout from the pandemic; many have indicated that more fiscal measures are likely. We are also hearing that China, which has been immersed in this crisis for many months now, is beginning to see a decline in the number of reported cases. This is definitely reassuring, but if you are invested in the stock market, you are still wondering what to do with your portfolio, which has definitely taken a whipping from this global market crash.

While we can agree that this may not be as bad as the 2008 financial crisis, it is starting to feel quite similar. In the last two weeks we have witnessed a 20 to 30 percent drop in some sectors, with unexplained one-way moves and huge intra-day volatility. While we know that our strong businesses will eventually lead us out of this recessive momentum, that change can't come fast enough to quell the panic. And even as we begin to see traces of the fear abating, the collateral damage is substantial.

Unfortunately, you only know what you know, as they say, and you can only control what you can control. The impact of this virus will be what it is, and we *will* come through it. The duration of this economic downturn cannot be predicted at this time, but if history has shown us anything, it is that this crisis, like all others, will pass and we will come out of it stronger and more resilient than before.

Let's first look at how the market dropped so quickly.

A perfect storm seems to have set the stage for the heavy negative price action seen early on. It began at the same time as the "quad witch" (short for quadruple witching) that occurs on the third week of each quarter; it is when the stock market generally experiences an increase in volatility due to stock options, futures, and contracts all expiring at the same time. This seemed to fuel a swelling of fear-based selling and we saw more and more price action that quickly turned negative. Traders could only stand back and watch in amazement as the deeply undersold stock began to bottom out some sectors.

On top of that, the following rapid-fire series of events hit the markets over the next five days of true "market panic":

March 10, 2020—Crude oil prices collapse (down 22 percent) due to lower demand and a battle for market share. Sources speculate that Saudi Arabia will increase production, which could lead to an oversupply that would take years to dissipate. (CNN Business)

March 10, 2020—Italy restricts movement and public gatherings; individuals are asked to stay inside. (*New York Times*)

March 11, 2020—The Bank of England cuts rates by 50 basis points to 0.25 percent in an effort to stimulate the UK budget. (Bloomberg and CNBC)

March 11, 2020—The World Health Organization declares COVID-19 a pandemic, urging businesses and corporations to take action to contain the virus in an effort to avoid overwhelming health systems. (*Time*)

March 11, 2020—The NBA suspends its season; many other sports leagues follow. (NBA.com)

March 11, 2020—The Dow and the TSX drop 19 to 20 percent, marking a clear decline into a bear market. (*Financial Post*)

March 12, 2020—Broadway shuts down: the greatest disruption of its kind since the terrorist attack on the World Trade Center in 2001. (*New York Times*)

March 12, 2020—In an effort to calm markets, the US Federal Reserve announces up to $1.5 trillion in additional financial assistance. (CNBC)

March 12, 2020—Walt Disney World closes. (CNN Business News)

March 12, 2020—US President Donald Trump announces a thirty-day travel ban to most of Europe. (NBC News)

March 13, 2020—Italy goes into total lockdown due to widespread infection. (CNN)

March 13, 2020—Iran, a nation of eighty million, uses security forces to clear streets on lockdown orders. (Reuters)

March 13, 2020—The Federal Open Market Committee (FOMC) cuts policy rates by 100 basis points, with a target range now at 0 to –0.25 percent. (CNBC) (The rate later moved back to zero, which was the same level it had been at from December 2008 to December 2015.)

March 13, 2020—The US House and administration agree on an economic stimulus package for food programs and unemployment benefits. (*New York Times*)

March 13, 2020—Trump declares a national public health emergency due to COVID-19. (CNN)

March 13, 2020—The European Union enforces strict travel bans as it learns that France has now joined Italy and Spain in full lockdown. (*USA Today*)

March 13, 2020—The Bank of Canada makes a surprising rate reduction to lower the central bank's benchmark interest rate by 50 basis points to 0.75 percent. (CBC)

March 13, 2020—Canadian Parliament rushes to pass US-Mexico-Canada trade agreement, and then later suspends it until April. (Reuters)

March 13, 2020—Canada's parliament is suspended until April 20. (CP24)

March 15, 2020—The US Fed, the Bank of Canada, the Bank of England, the Bank of Japan, the European Central Bank, and the Swiss National Bank announce a coordinated action to strengthen the US dollar. (*Bank of England Press Publication*)

March 15, 2020—Widespread school closures worldwide. (Global News Canada)

Economists now believe that overall global growth is expected to contract this year, and we are already seeing economists adjusting their Q1 and Q2 predictions. A global recession was declared on March 17 by Goldman Sachs and Morgan Stanley. (Fortune.com) So is this an environment you can still make money in? The answer is YES!

How to Use Today's Low Rates to Create Financial Freedom

I have said it before, and I want to say it here again: reviewing your savings portfolio is not the only thing you need to do during this time. Please take this opportunity to consider changing your debt portfolio to realize a lower rate for a longer term. The banks have been in a low-rate environment for almost twelve years, and once this pandemic passes and everything gets back to normal, they *will* want to raise rates. (As well as being an advisor, I am also a lender in Canada, and I have consulted colleges in the UK and the US. I can with all certainty tell you that just before COVID-19 became a pandemic, banks were planning to begin raising rates slowly. We were seeing posted rates back in the 5 to 6 percent range—of course, with discounts, but nonetheless, rates were beginning to rise.) This is the time to consider getting a new consolidation loan, to refinance your mortgage for a lower rate and longer term, or even to ask your banker if you can look at adjusting your student debts or other personal loans.

I know this could sound a little shallow, and perhaps even as if I want you to exploit the current economic situation—but that is exactly what I want you to do. In order to secure your future and ultimately retire debt-free and wealthy, you must take control of your debt and begin to build a plan to reduce it.

This pandemic is not being taken lightly by anyone, and although economists are trying to suggest historical parallels between this situation and SARS, the 2008 Financial Crisis, and 9/11, there is no real historical equivalent of this size and scale. Despite what you see and hear on social media, believe me when I tell you there *is* an opportunity for you in all this.

People who have read my columns and books or who have seen me speak know that I discourage people from continually refinancing debt into their mortgage. I will be the first person to will tell you never to use your home like an ATM to repeatedly get yourself out of debt. That said, rates are going to climb in the next couple of years and I would like you to get your debt portfolio in order now.

It is important to be honest with yourself. If you truly want to be wealthy you must be willing to do the things that will make you wealthy, which of course means eliminating your debt. You must establish a plan that enables you to live within your budget and save every month.

Why not use these extenuating events to review all your liabilities and set up a plan to pay them off by retirement? This will become part of the financial plan that we will do together in Chapter 4.

Buy Low: The Inevitable Market Rebound

Even though you may be filled with anxiety and worry right now, it is important to keep calm. There is usually a silver lining to these kinds of circumstances. We have seen the markets rebound many times in the past. It is important to remember that what goes down always comes right back up, especially when you are looking at the stock market throughout history. This pandemic truly is an unprecedented event that we are witnessing worldwide, and although we are currently seeing epic spikes in market volatility and a global stock market crash, I can guarantee you: this will indeed change.

When we find a vaccine for COVID-19 (which we will) and things slowly get back to normal, there will be an enormous amount of pent-up demand worldwide that will catapult our economies, businesses, and commerce to higher highs than we saw before this crisis. Looking at the last hundred years, some facts are just undeniable. The stock market is very "aggressive-reacting" and "regressive-reacting," which means it swings excessively to one side or the other at what might seem like breakneck speeds. We have seen the markets endure countless wars, epidemics, and major shocks, and it has always reached significantly newer highs than before each crisis— often highs we never thought possible. The markets will get through this, too, and—to put it bluntly—there may be a lot of money to be made if you invest when the market is down.

If you are (like many) thinking that all your money is now gone when you look at your investment portfolio statements, take heart: it isn't really gone unless you sell, so please don't sell! It will come back—I guarantee it. I know the markets are tumbling into double-digit losses, but that is exactly what happened with all the past market crashes. We've seen this over the last one hundred years we've been tracking volatility. So many people cashed out of their portfolios during the 2008 financial crisis, taking a huge financial haircut when they panicked and sold; months later they wondered just how to get back in again to recoup their losses—of course, at a much higher stock price than when they'd sold.

Why not see this as a stock market "sale" event. Talk to your advisor and see if this new market landscape is something you can take advantage of. Your advisor may call this a "tactical asset allocation," which means using a unique event or opportunity to purchase stock at an undervalued cost. (It is important to always seek professional guidance, especially during these times of market uncertainty.) This is the time to buy stocks that are at record low prices and a great value. Don't be short-sighted when investing for the future. Consider the long-term advantages of buying into the market at low price points to capitalize on future profit when the market turns again. While we can't say that we are out of the continued downward trend of equity markets, the sharp sell-offs will soon dissipate and markets will begin to rebuild.

Tip: When you are looking to get into a very volatile, downward-swinging market environment, it is hard to know when it has bottomed out. Resist the urge to try and time the market. This is virtually impossible and extremely difficult even for the most experienced traders. If you do decide to buy in and your portfolio goes down further, just leave it. It will come back up. Often, going in and out causes you more stress and leads to actual losses. If you want to know when to really get in, a "trader's tip" is to buy in when the stock market has had three full consecutive days of increases. This will mark a shift in the sell-off momentum, and although it may go down a little later, it is usually viewed as a sure sign of improvement and recovery.

The Best Investment Strategies Today

The announcement from the global central banks that they will provide unprecedented monetary stimulus provides greater flexibility to financial institutions to deploy capital that will help households and businesses meet their commitments. *The Wall Street Journal* reports that the European Central Bank plans to buy up to €750 billion in government and private sector bonds and corporate loans, and will assist with buying fixed-income securities.

If you are investing today, there are a couple of very good strategies to consider. If you prefer to stay clear of the stock market, I would suggest you definitely consider real estate. Real estate has long been considered one of the oldest ways to make money, and I have many very wealthy clients who have made their fortunes in real estate and never invested a dime in the stock market.

It is believed that with the low interest rates now on offer from banks, more and more people will enter the housing market; some predict a 10 percent growth in the market by the fall of 2020. The housing market increase we witnessed in 2017—the kind most economists say only comes around every twenty-five years—may indeed come again. It is predicted that rates will stay low just long enough to push first-time buyers back into the market and create a domino effect. We may not see huge increases in house prices, but they will definitely go up again. A rebound in the markets is anticipated around June and July with an increase to the real estate market later this year.

Buying investment properties and dealing with the maintenance and constant issues with tenants is not for everyone. Most people do not want the added debt or stress in their already full lives. If that is the case, why not consider an upsize—or maybe, instead, a "right-size?" That is when you move to a better area, a better property, or a better home to increase your home value over time. Let's face it, shelter is a necessity of life, but that doesn't mean you can't make money on it. This is one of the easiest ways to improve your family's lifestyle and your long-term financial resources. If your home has reached its top value and is only going up slowly year over year and you would like to improve your situation, now would be a good time. Take advantage of continued low mortgage rates and buy what you can afford to capitalize on the current situation.

For others who see this as a great opportunity to start investing in the stock market—I would definitely agree with you.

Please make sure to do your homework here and definitely seek the advice of a licensed advisor who has your best interests at heart. Find out what their value proposition is. Interview more than one and make sure you find a good fit with not only the advisor but also the brokerage firm.

Whether you are currently investing or just beginning, I want you to consider a product you may not have heard of yet: one that has just opened up to the average investor in the last five years. Most everyday investors are still just choosing a guided stock portfolio, exchange-traded funds (ETFs), or mutual funds. These are fine, and if you are happy with them, I would say keep going. But if you would like to consider something different, why not use what we have been offering our very-high-net-worth clients for decades? The product we recommend is called an SMA or Separately Managed Account. This is an institutional investment strategy that, in the past, was always reserved for large pools of capital like pension funds, research or hospital foundation moneys, large corporate and private investors, and even insurance pools of capital.

Essentially what they are is a collection of stocks in different sectors, managed by a highly skilled institutional money manager with the sole purpose of ensuring downside market protection (protective measures in place for limiting large market declines), a compounded growth structure, and capital preservation. Long touted as the number one investment in the UK, US, and Canada, SMAs have always been available only to the wealthy because a large amount of money ($500,000 and up) was necessary to get into the fund, or even to essentially mirror your portfolio to match an institutional money manager's segregated portfolio. I am glad to say that in the last five years the entry thresholds have been lowered substantially, and in the last three years they have become available in every sector—domestic, foreign, global, fixed income, and equities.

These portfolios have fared the best in the wake of COVID-19 and most will probably provide even higher returns than the typical mutual fund or ETF that the average person chooses online or at their bank. On the next page is a list of a few SMA portfolios that you can ask your advisor about. Again, do your research, know what is out there, and be smart about investing. Remember that the three killers to any stock portfolio are: 1) interest, 2) fees, and 3) risk. An SMA should ensure that you limit all three: they have some of the lowest fees in the industry; some will provide a guaranteed floor return value with growth projections; and all will limit the impact of a declining portfolio by lowering volatility.

SMA Funds to Consider:

Beutel Goodman SMA	Wedgewood SMA	Franklin Bissett SMA
Guardian SMA	Mawer SMA	Sionna SMA
Connor, Clark & Lunn SMA	Brown SMA	Montag & Caldwell SMA
Ashfield SMA	Brandes SMA	Epoch SMA
Walter Scott SMA	Kempen SMA	Sovereign SMA
Reaves SMA	Gannett Welsh & Kotler SMA	

Leveraged Lending Strategies

Leveraging means borrowing money, often writing off the interest based on what the funds are used for, and then investing in something that we feel will give us a higher return than the amount we are paying in interest on the borrowed funds. When most people think about leverage lending they imagine taking out a margin loan on their stock portfolio to buy more stock. While that is one method, I would actually caution you greatly to not do that, even now. There is a right way and a wrong way to use leverage lending, and unfortunately most people have only heard the horror stories about leverage lending and quickly dismiss it as a wise way to make money. Put simply, it is taking on more debt—and you should always be careful when you consider going more into the red. That said, wealthy people always have debt in their portfolios and are always on the lookout for opportunities to either invest, purchase, or transfer funds from investment to investment to build wealth.

If you think about it, do we not leverage lend when we buy a home? Most of us could never come up with the cash to cover the entire cost of purchasing a home, and anyone who can probably doesn't need to read this book. Rather than try to save the entire amount, we put down a little, take out a leveraged mortgage on our primary residence, and pay it off over time, right? So what is the difference? The difference is that the home is an appreciating asset, and we are generally assured that it will go up in value over time. Also, in most cases we are not just paying interest but, little by little, making a dent in our debt with every payment we make.

So in truth, leveraged lending done the right way does indeed build wealth.

I know a lot of readers would like me to condone borrowing to invest in the stock market, especially since it is down so low. Unfortunately, I can't. While I'm confident it will turn and go high, I can't predict when this will happen, and there are no real assurances it actually will—yet. I would prefer you invest in something a little more tangible such as real estate, an investment property, or maybe yourself.

Yes—*you*!

This pandemic has us all in a flutter, but it also has us all now thinking about our lives, our families, our jobs, and our futures as we adapt to the new "normal." Why not leverage yourself? You are a sure-fired exceptional risk to bet on, guaranteed. Use this new low-rate environment to help fund your dreams if you need to, and don't worry too much about the market right now. It will come back stronger than ever.

Having said all that, if you regularly invest in the stock market as part of a routine savings strategy, now is definitely not the time to sit on the sidelines. Some of you may use the ever-popular investment strategy of "dollar-cost averaging," which is to invest in the market with the same dollar amount each time on a set schedule, usually bi-weekly or monthly. The concept is to randomly buy stock at varying price points, which reduces the overall cost base of the portfolio, ensures that you contribute on a regular basis, and eliminates the need for market timing. Many people invest this way, and I have to agree that this is a simple and low-risk strategy if you want to set up a savings plan. Remember that the best days of the market usually follow the worst days, and dollar-cost averaging always tends to win in the long run.

HOW TO SECURE YOUR FINANCIAL FUTURE

ONCE THE COVID-19 CRISIS IS OVER, WHETHER THAT IS IN A few weeks or a few months, things will definitely get back to normal. Why not use this time to make a plan to reset your finances and to create some objectives or a target to improve your current situation? Remember that life is not a sprint; it's more like a marathon and it's important to stack the odds in your favour so you can enjoy the journey. With that in mind, there are a few fundamental tasks you must begin to master in order to increase your wealth so you can eventually retire comfortably.

I often see clients holding themselves back by living in the past, ruminating on and worrying about things that are out of their control. The secret to success is really not that difficult. You simply need to focus on managing your future. Break through your fear of not having enough money and stop limiting yourself. If you want to have more than you have right now to ensure a comfortable retirement, you need to invest the time and energy to get in the game and get on with it.

I am not asking you to defer happiness until you are retired. Instead, I want you to start making yourself happy now by improving your financial situation and providing more opportunities for your family and for your own personal growth.

So let's get started. Here are five foundational steps that are crucial to ensuring that you reach your new monetary goals.

1. Create a Lifestyle Budget

The number one thing older clients need is security, and that should really be the same for you now, no matter what your age. Security can be achieved by saving during your working years to build a financial portfolio that provides a solid foundation for the future. So how do you begin to save?

First, you must find out exactly what your current lifestyle costs. You can use the table you started in Chapter 1—but this time I want you to get a lot more detailed. Get a piece of paper and make a list of all of your monthly expenses and debts on one side of the page, and then on the other side list your monthly income. Is there enough? Can you pay all your monthly expenses without turning to credit? Are there funds left over to save, and if not, are there things you can cut out, compromise, or change to begin saving?

When you do not have enough money month to month, it is hard not to feel helpless. It may be necessary to give yourself a personal intervention to begin turning things around. Please do not be unwilling to make the necessary changes to begin saving. That will only prolong and perpetuate the problem, limiting your future and eventually making you more miserable. You need to start concentrating on managing your future. Leave the past in the past, with all the regrets and memories of broken plans. Start today to make the necessary changes in your life or career, and begin a new lifestyle budget to take control of your saving. Of course, as you move forward, you may have the odd setback. That is to be expected. But saving and planning for the future will provide you with the feeling of empowerment that will take you on to greater accomplishments in every aspect of your life.

2. Limit Your Bad Debt

There is a difference between "good" debt and "bad" debt. Good debt is what you take on to acquire an appreciating asset such as a home or an investment; you could even argue that school debt is good debt, because it will ultimately increase your long-term earning potential. Bad debt is debt collateralized on a depreciating asset or on revolving credit; it includes car loans, lines of credit, and credit card debt carried month to month.

Bad debt can be a killer! Having too much credit that you can easily dip into limits your ability to save, and it weighs you down with monthly payments that eat away at your bottom line. I know you are going to say your car loan is an inevitable expense, and I would agree with you. However, overextending to purchase a vehicle that is really out of your budget is not good. You know what you can afford, and having a conscious intention to not overextend and to embrace the mantra "live within your means" is really all I am asking here.

Bad debt does absolutely nothing to improve your financial situation; it decreases your cash flow, holds you back, and generally gives you no future opportunities to earn money, save, or increase your net worth. This worldwide pandemic has made us all reflect and take stock of our lives. The key to building wealth is not just saving; it is also taking the steps necessary to reduce your overall indebtedness. You may need to think outside the box to find those solutions.

Make a plan to eliminate your bad debt—pronto!

3. Invest Your Savings

In Chapter 1 I briefly mentioned the importance of monetization, but what does that really mean? Monetization is to convert, change, or exchange money. In banking terms, that is when you invest money into a secured asset platform over a set period of time to realize a guaranteed gain when cashed out.

Once you have established a savings portfolio, you need to get your money making more money. That is done by investing in the stock market or in real estate, or perhaps by simply contributing to your company's savings or pension plan. Don't get too fancy here. You do not have to invest in some high-tech product or employ a complicated strategy to feel like you are in a better position to monetize your money. Often, the simplest way of doing things is the best. You want to start saving systematically, and often the easiest way to get started is to have a set amount deducted from your income automatically. As I've already mentioned, you can also consider investing in property, buying a rental property, or simply upsizing your primary residence. There are also many government-assisted saving plans that can be a great way to invest. Bottom line: you want to start with tangible saving strategies that have limited risk and then move into other methods when you are feeling more comfortable with your asset accumulation.

Tip: When you begin to build an investment portfolio, resist the urge to use your home as your only source of retirement savings. Even though its value may mean your home is your biggest financial asset, be careful. Relying solely on your equity could leave you with less than you expect if the market declines drastically. Wouldn't it be nice to have other sources of income that mean you don't have to sell your home when you retire?

4. Keep Track and Keep Planning

Continually analyze your net worth to monitor your ongoing saving success. Your net worth is your financial snapshot; it measures growing assets against personal debt. You should assess your net worth every six to nine months to ensure that it is increasing year over year. Consider partnering with professionals who will help you get where you want to go. Get a good lawyer, a skilled accountant, and a trusted advisor who can assist you in planning your future. Remember: you don't know what you don't know. Acquire the knowledge you need to improve your financial situation. Create new financial habits that will help you wipe out your debt and reach your goals. I guarantee that your stress will dissipate when you begin to increase your net worth, and a feeling of confidence and comfort will inevitably bloom.

5. Estate Planning—The Last but Most Important Step

Good estate planning means planning for the inevitable, and making a Will is one of the most important and most responsible things you can do to ensure your hard-earned assets are taken care of according to your wishes when you die. You do not want to leave it up to a stranger at a government or state office to make decisions for your family. If you have children, it is even more critical to protect your estate for them and to have some say in their future care. You should also consider getting a Power of Attorney document drawn up in case you are unable to look after your own financial matters, and have an Advance Medical Directive prepared in case you are unable to communicate your needs during a health crisis. This is your opportunity to leave your mark! Don't forget to plan for your death when you are planning for your life. A Will gives you complete control.

Insurance is another part of the planning puzzle that can ensure you are protected against unexpected negative circumstances. Most people know that they need to have life insurance, but the average person typically does not have enough insurance, either because of the cost or because they think nothing will happen to them. Review your insurance coverage to make sure you have the proper policies to protect yourself and your family. Speak to a professional, and always have a separate policy outside your employer's plan. If you are laid off or change jobs after the current pandemic is over, you need to ensure that you are protected. Usually, peace of mind can be obtained at the cost of a daily cup of coffee—something you can easily squeeze into your budget for asset protection and debt elimination.

RETIREMENT STRATEGIES AND OPPORTUNITIES

THE COVID-19 PANDEMIC HAS GIVEN US ALL TIME TO THINK: it's provided a forced slow-down and a "pre-retirement" wakeup call. For those of you who do not have young children in need of constant care, but who have been somewhat isolated at home as you do your part in "social distancing," you've now had a glimpse of what it would be like to be home all the time—in other words, retired! So what do you think?

This is the time to start thinking seriously about how you want to spend your time in retirement. How do you envision your retired life and what do you want to do?

- Do you want to live in a rural area, in the city, or on the water?

- Should you consider downsizing sooner rather than later, buying a retirement home where you eventually want to end up, and renting it out for a few years before moving in?
- What are your personal aspirations?
- Do you see yourself in your current job until you retire?
- Should you consider investing in yourself to start a new business, go in a different career direction, or even go back to school?

Most advisors and pre-retirees believe planning for retirement should be entirely focused on the financial aspects of saving money and eliminating debt. While that is certainly important, there is so much more. How do you envision spending your time for the rest of your life? Retirement planning considerations should include finding meaning for your new life and fulfilling the goals you put on hold when you were working.

Tips to Help You Start Saving Now

Spending choices really do shape the world we live in. We have seen bottled water and toilet paper shortages, not to mention a shortage on cleaners, hand sanitizers, and face masks with the fear-based buying fuelled by the COVID-19 pandemic. There really is no actual need to hoard products at this point, but nonetheless it is hard not to feel the pressure to do so when you see others doing it.

It goes without saying that we really need to cut back on paid services and just try to do more things for ourselves. This includes cleaning services, lawn care, home improvements, and all those takeout meals we seem unable to live without. We need to get back to basics, and perhaps the pandemic will make us re-think our need to always have someone else do things for us.

To that end, consider some of the savings tips below and challenge yourself to come up with more. Think about how you spend your money every day and how you could make a difference that not only keeps the money in your wallet, but also helps the environment by being a little more "green."

- Stop buying new clothing and household items. Adopt a more "vintage" and eclectic style. Visit thrift stores; they offer fabulous items at a great price that can be "re-homed" and kept out of the landfill.
- Drive your car longer. Have regular maintenance and repairs done instead of trading it in just because the mileage is high or you have lost interest in it. Consider starting a carpool or taking public transit more. You will help the environment and reduce your expenses at the same time.
- Think about what you eat and drink. Start a garden and learn to freeze and can your fruits and vegetables. Pack your lunch and limit eating out to special occasions. Limit the specialty drinks and expensive snacks.

- Try to cut back the amount you spend on your pets. They honestly don't need fancy toys and would prefer your attention—which, by the way, is free. Consider cutting your pet's hair and nails yourself. Buying the right grooming tools is a one-time investment that will lead to future savings.

Creating Your Own Cascading Financial Plan

Creating a financial plan is vitally important for absolutely everyone—from a young person just entering the workforce, to someone in their forties or fifties, to someone who is already retired. You must have a plan for your life now and in the future. It must be personalized to you and your family, and must be written down with set goals and targets—and with a timeline to meet them.

We know things are going to change. It's inevitable. No one's life goes in a straight line. We all experience setbacks, hardships, and personal or career failures. But I want you to make a plan anyway. Most people do not do this; they wander aimlessly, allowing random circumstances to drive their actions, only to panic when something tragic happens. By having a plan you create a purpose, a goal to work toward, and you remove some of the uncertainty, which allows you to be more prepared in the future.

A financial cascading strategy to acquire wealth and protection is designed to flow into each decade of your life, with specific targets that you address every ten years. Of course, this is just a model plan; if you're behind on some of the suggestions, that's okay. The plan below is simply designed to provide you with a guideline to follow so you can begin planning for each ten-year milestone to ensure that you are on track for the future.

Cascading Financial Plan

20s: Career-building; becoming independent and moving out of your parents' home

- Acquire consumer and school debt
- Build up good credit history
- Buy into a participating whole life insurance plan

30s: Career-developing

- Begin building an emergency fund
- Begin saving for retirement and create a plan
- Invest in real estate and update insurance coverage
- Think about a debt repayment plan
- Have a Will and a Power of Attorney drawn up

40s: Career advancement or change; self-education and personal improvements

- Pay off all consumer debt
- Continue plans to build wealth, buy additional real estate, or add to savings
- Review insurance coverage

50s: Start de-cluttering and begin to live on less income

- Maximize savings strategies
- Work toward eliminating all debt/mortgages
- Think about long-term care coverage
- Limit risky financial ventures and monetary schemes

60s: Simplify your lifestyle and your commitments

- Downsize or right-size your residence
- Calculate your social security/pension benefits
- Reduce as much risk as possible in your investment portfolio
- Eliminate all debt and do not take on any new debt
- Update your Will and Power of Attorney

70s: Have a plan to fill your days

- Maintain or improve your health based on any new circumstances
- Nurture existing social relationships and build new ones
- Keep your brain active, read, and educate yourself
- Stay physically active (volunteering, gardening, painting, hobbies, etc.)

80s: Stay healthy; continue to be active
- Establish a support system and care directives
- Discuss your wishes with your family
- Plan for emergencies
- Stay involved, engaged, and—most of all—happy

The Benefits of a Collateral Charge— A Reason to Finally Get One!

A collateral charge is essentially a way for you to access the equity in a property if needed in the future, and is considered by most advisors to be a definite asset when planning for retirement.

It can be placed for 100 percent of the value of your property, and provides you the flexibility to borrow more funds if you need to in the future. All of the major banks now have some form of this product, but their offerings vary, so it is a good idea to review all the details before you jump in. This is considered to be a lifetime open lending tool, and clients can have multiple loan segments under their plan, which they can easily manipulate. Clients may choose to pay off their loans, set up new loans, or even change the terms, frequency, and amortizations of existing loans. This product provides many options for estate and financial planning and only needs to be registered once on the title to a property. I highly recommend this product for anyone who has good credit and owns their home. For the right client it is true financial freedom, giving them the flexibility to use the product as and when they see fit.

A collateral charge mortgage is available in the US, the UK, and Canada. Canada and the US do not use this product to its full potential, and that is a detriment to the average consumer. The internet offers a lot of information that discourages people from getting collateral charge mortgages; I would advise you to find out for yourself if this is the product for you. As an advisor to high-net-worth clients for many years, I can tell you that we have been using this product for decades; wealthy clients do not tend to want a traditional mortgage and prefer to have the added benefits that a collateral charge offers. I believe the negative attention toward this product has really been fuelled by mortgage brokers rather than consumers. Because this product has no term or renewal and is usually provided as an open lending vehicle, the old way of renewing your mortgage every three to five years can be eliminated— ultimately cutting out a steady stream of revenue for the average mortgage broker.

In my recent book, *How to Retire Debt-Free & Wealthy,* I show readers many ways to use a collateral charge to fast-track their debt, leverage lend, and even buy rental and investment properties. This product has many features and benefits that can help you build wealth and eliminate your debt faster. Speak to your banker and find out if it is right for you.

How Much Money Do You Really Need to Retire?

Well, isn't that a loaded question? It will be different for everyone, but it must be enough to at least make you feel financially comfortable and to provide for your security, freedom, and the ability to be independent as you age. Based on how you laid out your cascading financial plan, you should now have a good sense of how much you will really need.

In terms of an actual dollar amount you'll need by the time you retire, there is currently a basic benchmark: it should be in a long-term savings plan that you can draw on as you age, in addition to your government pensions. If you have an employee pension fund in addition to government benefits, you may not need to have the required investment portfolios listed on the next page. Of course, it would be great to have both, but one thing is for sure: you should have absolutely no debt when you retire. If that means you need to downsize to get rid of your mortgage or change your lifestyle to eliminate your debt load, then that is what you must do. Fear for your financial stability has no place in your future. Think of how much interest you will save by paying off your credit sooner. In most cases it equates to enough to pay for a new car or an extravagant vacation.

Minimum Projected Needs for Retirement:

Projection 1

- Employee pension plans, indexed for inflation
- Government pension benefits
- No debt
- No retirement savings

Projection 2

- Government pension benefits
- No long-term employer pension plan
- No debt
- Retirement savings = CAD$500,000 (USD$400,000; GBP£250,000)**

**These estimated investment savings projections are considered minimums for a retiring couple in today's currencies and should be invested for long-term compound growth to account for future inflation and taxation. Please note that these amounts are based on two people retiring together and sharing expenses. If you were to retire as a single person, with absolutely no additional financial support in the future, we would still recommend these amounts to ensure long-term financial independence, stability, and to cover future care.

Your Personal Retirement Test— Can You Retire Early?

Many people want to retire early and the thought of waiting until they are sixty-five seems like torture. So can you really retire earlier? For most of you, the answer is no. We just discussed how much money you really need for retirement, but of course, that will be different for everyone. Short of knowing when you will die, there is no real way to know whether you can retire early. One thing is certain: you must make sure you have a plan for the future and a retirement strategy to get there. This should be something you have considered carefully, and seeking the advice of a professional advisor or financial planner is always a step in the right direction.

Below are the twenty questions you need to ask yourself. Your answers will determine whether you can make a hard stop to commuting and say goodbye to the grind of your everyday work life. Be truthful with your answers; if nothing else, this will be a good exercise to help you understand what you need to work toward to retire earlier. Good luck!

1. Is all your debt paid off?
2. Are you really ready to give up working, or are you just tired of your current position and in need of a change?
3. Will you need to support anyone other than yourself? If so, for how long, and how much will that cost on a monthly basis?

4. Can you downsize your residence or move to a less expensive area to lower your expenses?

5. Will you have a consistent monthly revenue stream that is long-lasting and able to sustain you during times of uncertainty?

6. Can you create a revenue stream for yourself once you leave your traditional job or career (a home-based business or a new low-risk entrepreneurial investment strategy)?

7. Is this new revenue something that could last for many years, and could you continue to earn this revenue in your latter years?

8. Do you have any future large expenditures that you have not already saved for?

9. If necessary, could you make sacrifices to live a more minimalist lifestyle?

10. Have you made a financial budget for the future and can you write out exactly how you can, to the best of your knowledge, envision your retirement? How much do you anticipate this will cost in today's dollars?

11. Have you thought about inflation, taxation, and how you will ensure your investments grow securely with compounded growth year over year to ensure you do not run out of money?

12. Do you have a trustworthy team of advisors (lawyer, accountant, financial advisor, estate planner)?

13. Have you thought of ways to fill your time in retirement? What will you want to do day to day? What are your hobbies, your likes, your dislikes?

14. How will you keep your mind and body active in retirement?

15. When you are retired, do you plan to continue club memberships or join new ones, and how much will this cost?

16. How will you socialize in retirement and how much will this cost on a monthly basis?

17. Have you spoken to your partner about your plans? If you are retiring together, it is important to plan together!

18. Does your retirement partner want the same things as you, and are they willing to make the same sacrifices to retire now?

19. What are your plans for assisted living should you need care as you age? Have you calculated the potential costs and have you factored this into your savings?

20. Have you discussed estate planning with your advisor to account for taxation, inheritances, beneficiaries, and your wishes when you die? Do you have an updated Will and Power of Attorney?

Don't Stop Setting Goals!

In early retirement, sometimes referred to as "the honeymoon stage," early retirees feel like life is one long weekend with endless days of no alarm clocks, no meetings, and no deadlines. But once you have settled into a routine—then what? Goal-setting after you have retired is just as important as it was in helping you get there.

Start creating strategies to make your retirement more fulfilling and fun. Consider creating a legacy: pursue new things like art, literature, leisure activities, or even alternative work opportunities. Happiness is not attained just because you are retired; you are happiest when you're doing the things that matter most to you. Continue to dream and to seek inspiration. Everyone knows what they have come from, but many are not so sure what they are retiring to.

If you are widowed or divorced and are now on your own, all the more reason to look at your happiness beyond the financial aspects. Direct as much attention toward your new lifestyle issues as you do toward your new financial issues. This is your opportunity to refuse to be defined by some outdated image of retirement. We are in a modern and progressive era that welcomes uniqueness, innovation, creativity, and individualism. Plan to revel in your work-free days and make every day fantastic just for the sake of your own happiness. You deserve it!

TURNING LEMONS INTO LEMONADE

LET'S BE HONEST: THE ONE THING THAT IS TRULY HOLDING you back from reaching your ideal financial future is not this pandemic—it's you. Right now, I want you to change that. I want you to believe that you are worth more, and to stop believing that you "can't" attain more out of life. Holding yourself back is the worst thing you could ever do to yourself. Everyone has a unique and very personal vision of what they wish for their life. It may not be the clichéd wish for wealth and power. It could be a wish for a better relationship with a friend or loved one, for the ability to help others in a profound and thoughtful way, for a healthier lifestyle, for a career move, or even for a full-on life-altering change. Whatever your wish is, now is the time to begin to work toward your new future.

Keep a journal, write down your goals, create a workable plan, and make sure you really do it. You will be surprised at how even making a few small changes will make you happier and more successful in every facet of your life. Once you have begun to build momentum, you will find it easier to continue to move away from your old ways, and you will want more. Opportunities will become available to you that perhaps would have never been there before. You will find that with a simple shift in thinking, a willingness to try, and the determination to just do it, you will enrich your future and fulfill your true purpose in life.

Don't Underestimate Your Income Potential

Everyone needs an easy-to-maintain and realistic long-term strategy to become wealthier. Our natural instinct is to keep doing what we have always done and what is familiar. This is often referred to as the "definition of insanity"—doing the same thing over and over but expecting a different result. We all do this, not just with our finances but with our personal lives as well.

Remember the adage: "If you always do what you've always done then you will always get what you always got." I encourage you to make the necessary changes for the better and start stacking the odds in your favour. The fastest way for you to create more wealth is to believe in your ability to earn more. If that means you have to get a second job, go back to school to retrain, or change careers and get a better-paying position—then do it. Never underestimate your potential and always believe you are worth more.

New Beginnings—A Step in a Different Direction

Everyone has an "aha" moment when they finally say, "Okay, I am going to change. I'm going to go in a different direction, make a difference, and aspire for more." So what will spur you on to yours? This COVID-19 pandemic has forced most of us to slow down and smell the roses!

There are so many choices and personal opportunities out there and you need to plan your future in a way that allows you to become engaged and purposeful. Consider going deeper with your thoughts and ideas. Drop the negative beliefs that have always held you back, and stop selling yourself short. You really can do anything you set your mind to.

You can learn anything, be anything, and acquire the life you were born to live. I am not suggesting you can become a concert pianist if you have never played a note in your life, but maybe you can, if that is *really* what you want. You know what I mean here—sometimes all it takes is a concerted effort to let go of negativity to positively and persistently improve your situation. Everyone can have success according to his or her own unique definition.

Successful people fill their minds with all the ways to get what they want. I want you to start doing that—and no giving up this time. Believe you can, like yourself for making a change, and disregard the inevitable setbacks and obstacles that you will have to overcome in your journey. Just keep persisting until you succeed. You can go in a different direction, change your life, begin again. Just make a difference. All that is required is that you shift your mind toward believing that you can.

We Got This!

This pandemic has forced us to slow down, ponder our futures, and even look at some of the good things that have come from social distancing. Levels of air pollutants and carbon emissions over some areas of the planet have dropped significantly as COVID-19 has impacted our work lives and travel habits. Perhaps we will take this as a step toward truly mending our planet and making even greater steps to limit climate change.

For anyone who has lost a loved one, a friend, a neighbour, or a co-worker to this awful virus, you have my most heartfelt sympathy.

For anyone who is working on the front lines through this pandemic—health-care workers, truckers, law enforcement, and people working at grocery stores, pharmacies, and for delivery services—my sincere thanks to all of you for working every day to make sure we have the essentials to pull everyone through this crisis.

To those tirelessly researching to find a vaccine, my thanks as well. This is truly a challenging time for all of us. The upset, turmoil, and destruction that this pandemic has caused will never be forgotten, but like all things it, too, will be healed over with time.

We have all had to make sacrifices and modifications to our familiar routines, and I know many of you are very worried and fearful about your own health and safety. That is understandable and warranted, but please don't let this crisis turn you into someone you would not be proud of. Fear has a way of bringing out the worst in people. We have witnessed great kindness in some, but unfortunately, we have also seen some behave with a disturbing disregard toward others. Recognize that life, just like the financial market, has its highs and lows and we must always learn from the past in order to become more resilient, stronger, and ultimately more successful in every aspect of our lives. Make a difference. Be kind and forgiving, and be a good role model. Try every day to do the things that make your life more meaningful, more significant, and something you can be proud of.

We have all heard the sentiment "everything happens for a reason." I don't know if it's true, but sometimes it sure feels like it is. Perhaps it is our innate ability as humans to recover from tragedy, to fight through adversity, and to be ever-optimistic. If history is any indication, things will get better.

Nations have often found ways to come together to fix problems that affect us all. Countless times throughout history humanity has overcome wars, plagues, fires, earthquakes, and more; this pandemic, I believe, can also be overcome as we unite for the common good.

Perhaps all the social distancing and separation have actually brought us closer at a time when we all needed reminders to do the right thing, to slow down and appreciate what we have, to never stop believing in the power of our resilience, and of course—to always have hope for something better.

We got this!

ABOUT THE AUTHOR

CHRISTINE IBBOTSON has been providing financial advice to clients for over twenty-five years and is a Licensed Financial Advisor, Residential and Commercial Mortgage Broker, and Insurance Broker. She also attained her Chartered Investment Manager designation with further studies taken in Advanced Estate Planning, Trusts, and Taxation Strategies. Christine writes a syndicated column for over 360 community newspapers called "Ask the Money Lady" as well as another syndicated column focused solely on retirement called "Your Money Today" and recently published her first book, *How to Retire Debt-Free and Wealthy*. She continues to speak and provide advice to spread the ideas, tricks, and techniques of how everyday people can easily dissolve their debt, invest, and retire wealthy. Find her at askthemoneylady.ca.

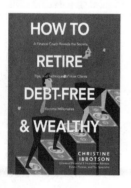

Also from Licensed Financial Advisor, Christine Ibbotson a narrative how-to guide focused on helping readers achieve their retirement dreams.

How to Retire Debt-Free and Wealthy
272 pages, $24.95 CAD
ISBN: 978-1-77108-802-2